Brettanomyces

poems by

Kelly Allen

Finishing Line Press
Georgetown, Kentucky

Brettanomyces

ACKNOWLEDGMENTS

To my family: my mother, whose buoyant encouragement never once
flagged, my father, who gave me the space and time to craft, and to my sister,
whose tireless drafting inspired my own.

To my good friend Eric, who supported my work with kindness and humor.

To all those whose left their mark in passing upon my life and my work:
Richard Ashton, Doug Fabbioli, Mike Musgrove, Darcy Ryan, John-Paul
Cheski, Eva Swidler, Laura Gerwin, Rob Blais, Keith Madden, Andrew
Sakach, Neal Wavra, Thad Parsons, Ben Sedlins, Eric Hoefler, Cathy Hailey,
Chase Bricker, Marth Becktell, and Greg Box.

Lastly, to Andrew. Thank you for giving me the paper beneath my feet.

Publisher: Leah Maines
Editor: Christen Kincaid
Cover Art: Kelly Allen
Author Photo: Andrew Lewis Napier
Cover Design: Elizabeth Maines McCleavy

Printed in the USA on acid-free paper.
Order online: www.finishinglinepress.com
also available on amazon.com

Author inquiries and mail orders:
Finishing Line Press
P. O. Box 1626
Georgetown, Kentucky 40324
U. S. A.

Table of Contents

The Winemaker's Apprentice

You asked me
is my heart in the grapes?
and you left those words
dangling like a lure,
Or an ultimatum.

Say no, and…well…
I felt your blade on my throat, shaking,
Poised like the sharp edge
of your pruning shears,
gaping against the neck of an unruly vine.

You weren't asking about the grapes.

When I told you that
I'm an opportunist,
That *this is the best chance I have,*
You made a snap decision
to prune or keep me.

Months later,
We sat face to face,
the same shears cool as ice against my jaw,
you asked the same question.
Say anything, anything at all.
Just don't say nothing.

I had
no words.
The metal bit like a viper.
Cutting me out.
I never saw you again,
never did have a chance
to answer your question.

My heart wasn't in the grapes.
It was in you.

Blood Terroir

The corkscrew blade hooked
around the neck of his wrist,
peeled back the foil of his skin,
His eyes on me as the vein drained flat,
Handing me the glass, he said:
"You never chill a red."

I promised him an heir but
never could deliver—
Couldn't carry myself through the crush.

When the grape press spewed its froth
like a beached whale,
I shuddered under a rain of pits and skins.
When I hugged frozen arms of cabernet,
chilblains smoldering,
black as the charcoal pyre of cropped canes,
When he chased my footsteps
through the ocean of the tasting room,
only to find me petrified,
reedy as a laurel tree.

He, the press,
He, the vine,
He, the room,

Accusation:
I, corking the syphon of his transfusion,
a sangoire stain coagulating in his lungs,
pressing like a bellows beneath my chest,
Under the vintage signature, his words pulled
Like bitter acid from the profile *terroir*:
"Finish the job."

Holding his heart by the stem,
The blood struck like a match—
Zero Brixx.
I pressed the glass to my lips,
And he burned.

Tannic

She sits in his belly,
The oak staves of his barrel chest
Trapping her like a cask.
A tongue like a lash,
wrapped, soft as velvet, around her wrists,
Decanting, breath by quaking breath,
The tannic infusion of her palate.

Condensation beads along her hips
running like tears in glistening macramé,
His body breaching the chill on her glass shoulder,
He swirls her in his palm,
Leans her back by the stem,
Tracing her legs towards the lip.

That parched kiss,
Green as a spring cabernet—
Her lips are leathery cassis,
Frigid astringency,
easing under the sweet tobacco
Of his charcoal embrace.

Blush rosé smolders down
A languid dispersal of anise smoke,
Plumy embers of nutmeg spice
burning like a blindfold.
In the dark terrarium of his iron arms
Phantom vines creep towards wisps
of oxygen slipping through his fingers.

The distillate of her second *anthesis*,
Is a parceled *gout de terroir*,
Ripening under honeyed trefoil canopies,
Never ridding herself
of that grassy quince complexion,
Of berries plucked too soon.

Brettanomyces

She walked out of a drought
and into a wine bottle,
Shells of foil cappings
Crunching like shucked oysters
Beneath her feet.

Like an abandoned flag,
She leaves her name at the cork,
Assumes that of the oracle,
Brettanomyces,
The Dark Angel.

Ghosts move like marionettes beneath your fingers
Drunk with glamour and verdant mythos.
Reincarnation is a tasting of verticals,
Each vintage has its tarnish,
each, a transcribed *Loka*,
driving us up and down these zipper straits
of this Dharmic multitude, this
Uncorked diaspora.

All of it spun like gilded thread
into the glassen spools lining your cellar.
The immortal sarcophagi
of your manifold faces.

Until you see her.
The fatal inoculation,
At the capitulate of her own brevity,
A residual aeration, slipped from
pursed lips,
just another gust of wind,
rolling down the alleyway
between the curve of the glass
and the deep sleep of the bottle.

Teacher

I uncork the bottle,
see a sickle line split your wrist,
And swift your blood,
decanting like Delphi's sacrament
atop the vineyard soil.

The springing vines that come
are black with thorns,
roses by other names,
a poetica lexicon, bound raw
and primal by taste and tongue alone,
This thing you painted to life,
a drunken language, oracular.

I smell it, sweet on my breath
and hot beneath my skin, set fast,
red as the blood you fed it,
a fated yarn pulling me into a tundra
of unmarked bottles,
atmospheres held under *muselet*,
decades embalmed and of partaken,
the vampiric cannibalism of the public,
syphoning your labors with their daily bread.

Do they come away enlightened?
Or dully stupefied by the open hourglass
Christening their table?

Kissed Burgundy, the air blushes bittersweet,
Colored by the tune of the pour,
I drank your rhetoric
And now fluent, I speak it just as red.

The Graft

The graft is a lobotomy.
A weak seam where bulging cankers and
Crumpled goiters congest into malformed hemispheres,
Two parts fused in a slip knot:
This fragile *Flora collosum*.

Jointed, a spare arm stretches skyward,
Breaks its wrist on the steel cordon,
Heals,
With stiff fingers cropped
Into sighing lock-jawed wind catchers,
Postured upright by a trellis corset.

But below the graft, knock-kneed limbs
Spit out in tongues of frilly sage,
Little flames licking the scandalous, shabby ankles.
No one guessed about the rootstalk,
Until the cagey sprouts snapped the high wires,
and dried into a round, tawny crackle.

Damned Russian Thistle,
Beating its wings.

Come autumn,
All of that docile *Vitis vinifera*
Slid into that leaky, severed space,
Where the flighty rootstalk
Chewed itself clean out of the earth.
Witnessed under a stinging, pearly freeze,
The whole vine shook loose
and just tumbled away.

Salmagundi

Sipping on the salted edge of my sober world,
I see you, tracing the grooves left
by the tailored melody of your meticulous handiwork
Shaken glasses, your
clouded sky eyes,
the circlet of your twisted bar spoon,
double helix whorling like a stormcloud over ice,
Stainless strainer, wire coils like the dead artery of a lightbulb,
 waiting for the torch.

The vortex of the shaker, clasped,
hand on either side,
circulating truth and glamour,
like a siren's call.
The marimba, the guiro,
the percussive bid for truth.

Mixology is a mirrorwork lanterna,
A salmagundi, delectable and precise in its artifice,
its recreation of a singularity from the gaudy shambles
of tongues and arms,
fingertips, and open palms,
of breathless lips,
parted like the infinite space between stitches
in your highball embroidery.

Suturing together the threadbare seams
of the burning out,
the basted and unfinished hems of men and women,
stacked like bolts of cloth along the bar,
in the sparkling flambeau
of your epicurean cocktail.

Congruency

Mathematician,
Enshrined within your *Illustratium*,
the Moorish symbology of your linear kingdom is a helixed bloodline,
A distillate syllabus, doubling like a switchback
In the patternry of your transversal flicker,
Truth, fined from numbers,
Is scalene firelight, equalizing every angle
Between us.

Whispering analogues
Shear along my tannic edge like the head of a match,
Petitioning the flame, the
generative solution,

I am in the business of whispers.
I peddle dreams.
This language is understood.

Winemaker...huckster,
Seamstress of potions, a soothsayer's *aqua vitea*,
My charlatan's rucksack is like a harness,
Chaining me to the earth, these liquid baubles,
are tarnished tawny at the summit of the pour,
(They call that the *corona*, as if to say,
once celestial, now secularized)
Like a soul divested of its stuffing.

Parallel congruence.
Your coinage is truth, whereas mine is circumstance.
Calculating tessellations of ruby satire on pure hunch,
silver-tongued hints of the same maxim that your sorceric theorem
predicted long before the cork:
A baffled unity,
stricken dumb and ageless in its vertex.

Piano Wire

A dark thread sticks
where your fingerprint whorled my tongue.
You must have been tuning that old piano,
the one whose language you keep meaning to learn,
and pocketed a treble wire.
I can feel its cool silver against my throat,
choking back the words.
Holding down the mute.

You don't mean to.
The music gives itself away,
so,
you keep it spun up in noiseless threads,
carrying them beneath your nails,
where they wait to be translated
in the pounding rain of your,
our,
new language.

A language of quiets.

A language that has no words,
only notes.
A duet that we play,
a garrote that, like the bolts of your piano strings,
is slowly tightening around both of us.

Trace Discourse

My tongue feels like a scrimshaw Pollack,
The exchange of a genre tendered,
Chiseled out currency smeared like tarnish
Over lethal curiosity.

You at the steering wheel, I beside
Mirrored in a pollen-caked windshield,
Our eyes meet,
And the cab is a crackling snare, clamping me down.

Your:
Hand outstretched presses like a sigh.
My:
Baited glance cleaves at the uncut stone,
Sheer glass between each word.

A pattern unfurls like a blossom across your palm—
Caught breath swallowed in a confession,
Behind pocketed fingertips.
Our trackless playbook cutting like the switchbacks
Of the mountain we're climbing,

Mt. Rainier rises like a heavy minaret
above toothy conifers and a cabin we share
(with three others, packed like our luggage in the rear seats)
Come sunset, we'll sit with a bottle each by the lake,
devised equilibrium—keeping our hands and mouths full.
There can be no parting discourse here.

Your eyes pin me like a wire trap,
My voice leaves no trace in this profane, Cascadian Eden,
Just my paint-stained nailbeds,
Scratching at stagecraft,
And your untenable entreaty
tasting thin as the clay dust
Veiling the mountain air around us both.

Voice on a High Wire

On my narrow inch,
sliding along your fingerprint copula,
Every word is a ripple under my feet,
Wrinkles cobbling my high wire,
Stumbling over and over,
like a needle
skipping along the same vinyl ditch.

This braille underfoot,
your untranslated watermark,
Presses like an invitation.

Let quake by the half-life of your deeply aerated lure,
my cable trapeze
plucks a gasp through my ribs,
As I wobble on the precipice
Of this suspended garland whisper.

Tracing now the sumptuous brush
Of sweet persuasion against my skin,
This tight strand underfoot murmurs
Like an afterglow,
And I am wondering
Where your fingertips lead.

Sign Language

A flourish of neat fingers,
whisking the air like fluttering shrapnel.
Those gentle blades,
slipping into me as seamlessly as needle-drawn thread
In your silence, talking not with lips,
But pressure,
Tidal sign language rushing like a pulse over my skin,
written like an unsanctified contract,
impermanently signed with still-warm ink
cooling inside of me.

Amidst the hazy fallout of rumpled cotton sheets,
Echoes of a shattered memory expel, piecemeal:
Purple fingerprints like resigned tattoos,
My arms, a dim script of blooded ink.
I'm buckled in the corner, crumpled under the stains
Of his endless revision—
With every draft, I'm sheared in two.

The chilly brail of gooseflesh
prickles beneath your touch,
a hematic mirage, resurrected
with your sign language alchemies.
Stale blood shuddering out of coagulation,
raising to the fountain nib.
Was it love, the ink in its pinched, narrow neck?

My paper body is a sheaf, a dossier,
Its bailiff a string of red corrections
bubbling up through a pale, blank dermis.
Your hands retreat, the drafted article prostrate
Incised and redacted, deeply, but not deep enough
To pull the blurry smudges
of his shredded first draft.

Aspen

Beneath her gauzy green frock,
stockings the color of unripe lemons pucker
a raw hem
like the unfurled sleeves of drying canvas.

Narrow veins etch their way
over her…
…under her,
wire twine stinting the reedy flute of her throat.
When the wind comes, wild hymnals quicken
her silver perch in a séance possession
filled with hollow music.

The air is a checkered sound.

An orbed waif rigid with tremor,
She shivers in a wash of chlorophilia.
Abraised by the gritted wind,
the ground beneath her feet
anoints with resinous juniper incense,
skinwalker blood of the arroyos.

Now she is holy.

Distant Rain Dance vibratos strum
the velvet of her belly and
she leans,
her long neck lolling at the crook.
A dangerous angle,
the sacrificial aorta of the spirit rudely bared
to an irradiated New Mexican sky:
The azure ax above.

Look! Look! Look! Look!

Wracked by the lyrical garble
of oily, pandering ravens,
a razor white wind yields in flight
from the knobby bald,
The near-kiss of snowfall
Rolling over her like a shuddering sneer.
Clutching helpless to the parchment bark,
Her hobbled stem trembles,
expecting the gilded fall.

Coyote

Coyote, coyote, maul of the desert,
tripling paws skitter,
sandstone bluffs *tack-tacking* under ragged nail,
a speckled trace of dribbled saliva
evaporating like pictograph wraiths in the turquoise twilight.

Coyote…coyote…
Your yipping, lopping cry,
staccato bark and branching wail, jaws stretched
as though in thirst of rare raindrops,
your artful tenor is strange chamber music.
Pinion breath, smoke-touched,
The earthy cigarette in your paw is my nostalgic incense,
or was it the iron tang of stale blood on your curling lips
that made my mouth so dry?

Howl like a fae reel,
Prickly sloe liquor lapping at my southern soul,
I met you first cantering over my heartstone,
In the Arizona red rock and ruddy Virginia clay,
High up in the candid streams and green tunnels
of my ancestral Appalachia.
A brooding mimesis of my cerebral interloper,
Two faces for two lands.

Your eyes laugh in dark coffee tones,
quietly jubilant vulpine,
wandering exhausted fields like a leper,
clabbering together fallen limbs,
plastering the sloughing fur of mange with auric numinosity,
the cradle of civilization was a shotgun down your throat.

Surface damage only,
With your crumbling eastern face diminished
to half-breeds and mutts,
the nilch'i fled through the sipapu in your chest,
up, up…
and into the next life.
Get up, get up coyote,
The garrulous leaves of autumn are calling,
And it's time for me to take you home.

Erasure

His percussive abuse,
Rakes toothy arroyos over her red face,
A bruised claw of heavy rain
battering her naked hills,
Trimming the fat from the lean
Of her jaw,
Carving out loose molars
From the pinky gums of her dry river mouth,
Her barren beds of sand, where the fish are as desiccated
As tamale husks
with blue corn eyes.

A fresh downpour of
Spittle on her chin,
Sticks like a glaze of pearly milk,
Rolled cellophane across red ochre palms
Haloed over her hips and thighs
And dark, deserted caverns,
A latex sheath stretched between
The petroglyph tattoos left by faded romances
(Whose lovemaking marked her in and out)
And this pale-faced, eastern sky
Turning her white with his bitter paint.

She bears him Three Sisters:

The first, she strips down and boils
Before the sweet fruits of her daughter's flesh
Part the green leaves of her skirt.

The second, she skins and hacks to pieces
Frying the body in bear grease and salt,
Squeezing fresh prickly pear juice
The color of spring blood
Over the remains.

The third, she abandons
in a field of parched yucca spears
Until there is nothing but a hollow rattle
full of dry bones,
And these she puts in an old glass jar
In a dusty corner where no one can see
The red of their Anasazi skin.

Each time the monsoon blows in
To bleach the shoulders of her eroding streams,
With its enameled crème.
She sees the shriveled beans of her
Butchered trinity
Shiver like the tippling of a leaning rain stick
In the silence of their glassy tomb.

Teeth

He tossed the underjaw at Creator's feet,
Where it hooked on the boarder like a horseshoe,
Black molars gnashing on a crust
Of sky so blue,
So blue,
Must be the last thing Creator saw
Before he died.

In the shadow of the teeth,
Black hunger slithered and wriggled
In the fingers of the People.
Creator made their eyes too dark to see
Brother Jackrabbit's mesquite fur,
Ears as pale as the bean tree,
Or Grandfather Bison's felted curls,
Two creosote eyes like drops of tar.

White man brought white things
To the charred teeth:
White sugar in a white paper sack,
White grease in a white-top tin,
White lines on white-faced mirrors,
Brown reflections cut into rows
with razors.

Last thing White Man did
Before he killed Creator
Was rip out the stories
Tooth by tooth,
And lay them in a heap
Like kernels of parched blue corn
So the People couldn't find the words
For "eat."
For "live."

The People gobbled up White Man's sweet words,
And grew bigger,
Sugar syrup, thick as poison
In the blood,
Hungry for a taste of old Creator's stories,
Before White Man threw them away.

The Brass Telescope

I built a telescope out of brass,
though looking back,
I see now
that it wasn't brass at all,
only the red rock out beyond the property line.
It looked well enough and bent when I touched it,
so I made a telescope with it,
put on the butt of a wine bottle for a lens.
Green's a good color on you.

I built a telescope just so I could see you.
I keep changing around the setting.
First it's all watershed forests, craggy granite.
Then it's Ojo chamisa, pinion pine,
Rockrose, and Mormon Tea.

An experiment
Just for fun.
Sometimes I get it right,
Before I write down the trees and the brush,
I take a look through the glass
just to make sure I don't forget you.
Don't bury you.
Just in case you're there.

Sometimes,
I think you see the sun catching on the metal
and it scares you off.
You can't see that it's me
from so far away.

I took sandpaper to the sides to tarnish its sheen,
scratch off the shine.
It looks more like proper stone now,
and I don't get confused as often.
But the lens still looks
like the end of a bottle,
and it's hard to make out your face
through its mouth.

The Oxygen Mask

Take a deep breath and count backward from ten...

One
A Clarion seagull cuts the air in two with its guillotine cry.

Two
A pair of feet planted in a subzero rip tide.

Three
The sky is a dusty pearl.

Four
The shore is a broken zipper with its tail bobbing in the surf.

Five
Salt rash clings like an anklet at my heels.

Six
One step into the silted floor. My feet sink into the soundless nothing.

Seven
Eyelashes knit in damp crochet, matted tears tracing thick lines.

Eight
The rising tide is an iron maiden in my arms.

Nine
Oceanic collar, my dress is funerary sea-form boucle.

Ten
I can't breathe.

Following the culmination of a degree in Sustainability, Kelly Allen pinned her focus on revitalizing local foodways as means of resistance against cultural hegemony and the mechanization of individualistic expression. Tracing a path of agrarian incarnations in multiple small farms across the United States, Kelly worked alongside numerous Virginian and New Mexican sustainable homesteaders, ran a small CSA (community-supported agriculture) operation off the coast of Maine, and spent a season teaching sustainable arid-lands agriculture at the Institute of American Indian Arts in Santa Fe, New Mexico.

www.ingramcontent.com/pod-product-compliance
Lightning Source LLC
LaVergne TN
LVHW021127080426
835510LV00021B/3346